New Hampshire

BY ANN HEINRICHS

Content Adviser: Ann M. Hoey, M.A., M.S.I., Children's Coordinator, New Hampshire State Library, Concord, New Hampshire

Reading Adviser: Dr. Linda D. Labbo, Department of Reading Education, College of Education, The University of Georgia

COMPASS POINT BOOKS ✦ MINNEAPOLIS, MINNESOTA

Compass Point Books
3109 West 50th Street, #115
Minneapolis, MN 55410

Visit Compass Point Books on the Internet at *www.compasspointbooks.com*
or e-mail your request to *custserv@compasspointbooks.com*

On the cover: The Mount Washington Hotel and Resort in Bretton Woods, a national historic landmark

Photographs ©: Warren Stone/Visuals Unlimited, cover, 1, 21; John Elk III, 3, 31, 35, 36, 37, 47, 48
(top); Corbis/David Muench, 5; Ned Therrien/Visuals Unlimited, 6, 16; Chuck Swartzell/Visuals
Unlimited, 8, 22, 24; Robert McCaw, 9, 25, 42; Unicorn Stock Photos/Andre Jenny, 10, 19, 43 (top);
North Wind Picture Archives, 11, 14, 15, 28, 41, 45; Hulton/Archive by Getty Images, 12, 13, 27, 46;
Getty Images, 17; D. Yeske/Visuals Unlimited, 23; Corbis/Erik Freeland, 29; Bachmann/The Image
Finders, 30; Eric Anderson/Visuals Unlimited, 32; Richard C. Johnson/Visuals Unlimited, 34; Photo
Network/Nancy Hoyt Belcher, 38; Reuters NewMedia Inc./Corbis, 39; Sharon Gerig/Tom Stack &
Associates, 40; Robesus, Inc., 43 (state flag); One Mile Up, Inc., 43 (state seal); Gustav W. Verderber/
Visuals Unlimited, 44 (top); William J. Weber/Visuals Unlimited, 44 (middle); Photo Disc, 44 (bottom).

Editors: E. Russell Primm, Emily J. Dolbear, and Catherine Neitge
Photo Researcher: Marcie C. Spence
Photo Selector: Linda S. Koutris
Designer/Page Production: The Design Lab/Jaime Martens
Cartographer: XNR Productions, Inc.

Library of Congress Cataloging-in-Publication Data
Heinrichs, Ann.
 New Hampshire / by Ann Heinrichs.
    p. cm.— (This land is your land)
Includes bibliographical references and index.
Contents: Welcome to New Hampshire!—Mountains, valleys, and streams—A trip through time—
Government by the people—New Hampshirites at work—Getting to know New Hampshirites—
Let's explore New Hampshire!
 ISBN 0-7565-0336-1
1. New Hampshire—Juvenile literature. [1. New Hampshire.] I. Title. II. Series.
 F34.3 .H45 2004
 974.2—dc21   2002012866

Table of Contents

NOTE: In this book, words that are defined in the glossary are in **bold** *the first time they appear in the text.*

"Live free or die! Death is not the worst of evils."

Those are the words of New Hampshire's General John Stark. He was a hero in the Revolutionary War (1775–1783). Many other New Hampshirites shared Stark's bravery. They helped the American **colonies** win their freedom. Now, New Hampshire's state motto is "Live Free or Die."

New Hampshire had many industries in its early days. Water-powered mills grew up along the Merrimack River. Dense forests provided trees for shipbuilding. New Hampshire has kept up with the modern world. Today, its factories make computers and other electronics.

New Hampshire is a land of rugged mountains, deep valleys, and swift, sparkling streams. The White Mountains cover much of the state. Early settlers called them the Crystal Hills. Made largely of **granite,** they glistened in the sun. The mountains gave the state its nickname, the Granite State. Residents and visitors love its mountains, forests, and wildlife. Now let's explore New Hampshire. You're sure to love it, too!

▲ Birch trees and the White Mountains

▲ If you look closely, you'll see that Old Man of the Mountain resembled the profile of a human face. The profile fell off the mountain in May 2003.

New Hampshire is one of the New England states. It's located in the nation's northeast corner. Just north of New Hampshire is Canada. To the west is Vermont. Massachusetts is to the south. Maine is to the east. Southeastern New Hampshire borders the Atlantic Ocean.

New Hampshire is very small. It could fit into Texas twenty-eight times! Only six other states are smaller than New Hampshire in land area.

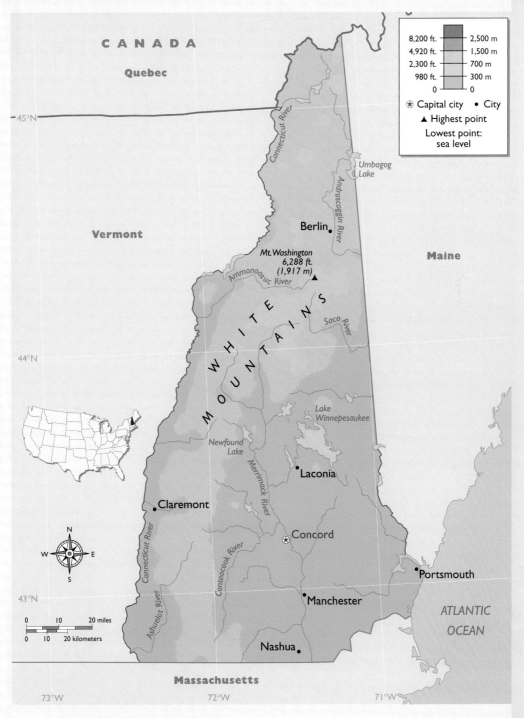

CANADA

Quebec

8,200 ft. | 2,500 m
4,920 ft. | 1,500 m
2,300 ft. | 700 m
980 ft. | 300 m
0 | 0

⊛ Capital city　• City
▲ Highest point
Lowest point:
sea level

45°N

Connecticut River

Umbagog
Lake

Androscoggin River

Berlin

Vermont

Mt. Washington
6,288 ft.
(1,917 m) ▲

Maine

Ammonoosuc River

W H I T E

Saco River

44°N

M O U N T A I N S

Lake
Winnepesaukee

Newfound
Lake

Merrimack River

Laconia

Claremont

N
W · E
S

Concord ⊛

Portsmouth

Connecticut River

Contoocook River

43°N

ATLANTIC
OCEAN

0　10　20 miles
0　10　20 kilometers

Ashuelot River

Manchester

Nashua

Massachusetts

73°W　　　　72°W　　　　71°W

▴ **A topographic map of New Hampshire**

Glaciers once covered New Hampshire. They carved out jagged, stony mountains and deep valleys. That created northern New Hampshire's White Mountains. They are the highest peaks in New England. Among them is Mount Washington, the state's highest point. Another peak, Cannon Mountain, is better known as Profile Mountain. Until a rock slide in May 2003, one side of it looked like the profile, or side view, of a human face. It was called the Old Man of the Mountain.

The Merrimack River runs down the southern half of the state. New Hampshire's three largest cities lie along the Merrimack. They are Manchester, Nashua, and Concord, the state capital.

▲ A Civil War monument in Nashua, one of New Hampshire's three largest cities

To the east and west are many hills and lakes. The Connecticut River runs down the western border. Both the Merrimack and the Connecticut valleys have rich farmland. Along the Atlantic coast are wetlands and sandy beaches.

Forests cover most of New Hampshire. They provide wood for the state's paper mills. Maples, beeches, pines, and other trees grow on the hillsides. People make maple syrup from the sweet sap of maples. Dwarf birch and willow trees grow high in the mountains. Muskrats, beavers, and snowshoe hares scurry through the forests. The largest animals are moose, bear, and white-tailed deer, the state animal.

▲ Snowshoe hares live in New Hampshire's forests.

Ocean breezes bump into New Hampshire's mountains. This often creates quick changes in weather. A day may start warm and end cold. Summer is usually cool. Winters are often cold and snowy. That's when skiers hit the slopes. Fall is a beautiful time of year. Then the leaves turn bright yellow, red, and orange.

▲ **Mount Washington Hotel and Resort in Bretton Woods is a popular place for skiers in winter.**

A Trip Through Time

▲ **Many Native American tribes lived in New Hampshire.**

Thousands of Native Americans once lived in New Hampshire. Two major groups were the Pennacook and the Abenaki. Both groups were made up of many tribes. They built their homes with wooden poles covered by bark or animal skins. In the forests they hunted deer, moose, and bears. They fished in the streams and gathered wild plants.

The Pennacook lived in farming villages along the Merrimack River. Their name means "at the bottom of the hill." In the summers, they moved to the seacoast. There they fished and gathered shellfish.

▲ Abenaki Indians inhabited northern New Hampshire at the time British colonists arrived.

The Abenaki lived farther north. Their name means "people of the dawn." They grew the four "sacred plants"—corn, beans, squash, and tobacco. They stored their extra crops in underground pits so they would have food for the winter. They were also good at making canoes and snowshoes. To the Abenaki, Mount Washington was a holy place. It was the home of the Great Spirit.

England began setting up colonies in North America. John Mason received land between the Merrimack and Piscataqua Rivers. Around 1623, Mason sent settlers to his land.

David Thomson set up a fishing village in present-day Rye. Edward Hilton settled at today's Dover.

This land joined the Massachusetts Colony in 1641. In 1680, the New Hampshire Colony was created. It would be one of thirteen American colonies. New settlers cleared trees and built homes in the wilderness. Native Americans taught them to grow pumpkins and squash.

▲ **British colonists in 1623 building a settlement at Odiorne's Point**

▲ **A New Hampshire family preparing a minuteman to go to war**

The **colonists** didn't like Great Britain's harsh laws and
taxes. They fought for freedom in the Revolutionary War. New
Hampshire sent hundreds of men to battle. They were called
minutemen. They were ready to fight at a minute's notice. In
January 1776, New Hampshire declared its independence
from Britain. It was the first colony to do so. It became the
ninth U.S. state on June 21, 1788.

New Hampshirites were opposed to slavery. They fought on the Union side in the Civil War (1861–1865). Shipbuilders in Portsmouth built strong warships. After the war, many new factories and businesses opened. Some made leather or wood products. Water-powered textile mills turned out cloth. Thousands of people came from Canada and Europe for jobs.

During World War I (1914–1918), New Hampshire's shipyards were busy. Shoes and other leather goods became a big industry. World War II (1939–1945) gave New Hampshire another boost. The state supplied boots, soldiers' uniforms, ships, and submarines.

▲ **New Hampshire sent troops to serve in the Union army.**

▲ **Hiking in the White Mountains is a popular tourist activity.**

Today, new industries keep New Hampshire strong. Its factories make computers and many other electronic products. Tourism is an important industry, too. Visitors love New Hampshire's rugged, natural beauty.

▲ George W. Bush greeted supporters in Amherst during the 2000 presidential campaign.

When it comes to government, New Hampshirites are experts. They were the first to declare independence from Britain. Today they hold the first statewide **primary** during presidential campaigns. Primaries are elections to pick each party's **candidate** for president. Candidates often pin their hopes on New Hampshire. If they win there, they're off to a great start.

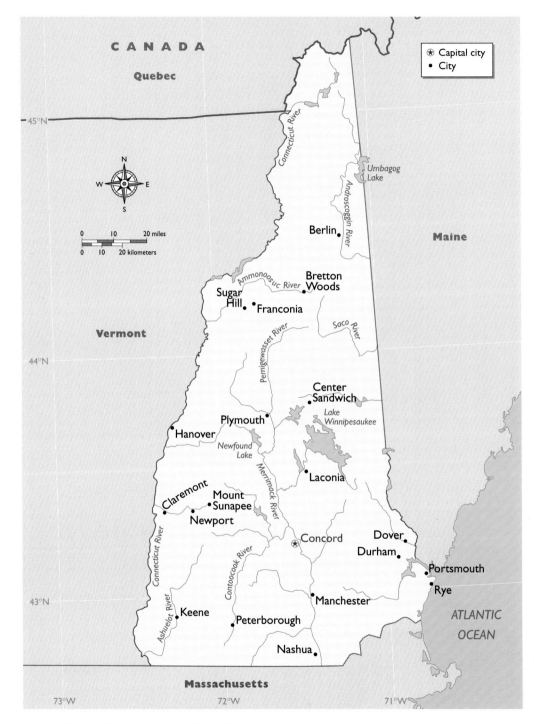

▲ **A geopolitical map of New Hampshire**

▲ New Hampshire's legislative branch meets in the state house in Concord.

Even children get involved in their government! Fifth-graders in Concord wanted the ladybug as their state insect. They wrote to their state lawmakers about the ladybug's fine qualities. Lawmakers had meetings and argued about it. Finally, the ladybug was voted the state insect.

New Hampshire's state government works like the U.S. government. It has three branches—legislative, executive, and judicial. The legislative branch makes the state laws. Voters elect lawmakers to serve in the state legislature, which is called the General Court. It has two houses, or sections. One is the 24-member senate. The other is the 400-member house of representatives.

The executive branch sees that laws are carried out. New Hampshire's governor is the head of the executive branch. Voters elect a governor every two years. That's a short time, but a governor can serve any number of **terms.** Voters also elect a five-member executive council. The council must approve any officer the governor appoints. The General Court selects the secretary of state and state treasurer.

The judicial branch is made up of judges and their courts. They decide whether someone has broken the law. New Hampshire's highest court is the state supreme court. It has five judges. All judges must retire when they reach the age of seventy.

New Hampshire has ten counties. Each county has a sheriff and other officials. There are thirteen **incorporated** cities in New Hampshire. Each one elects a mayor or manager and a city council. Outside the boundaries of those cities are 221 towns.

Democracy means rule by the people. Most of the country has a representative democracy. In that system, people elect representatives to stand for their views. Most of New Hampshire's 221 towns, however, have a pure democracy. Their citizens make decisions by voting in town meetings.

▲ **The town hall in Chesterfield**

▲ The old Amoskeag Mills buildings in Manchester now provide space for a wide range of businesses.

Textiles, or cloth, were once New Hampshire's major product. Manufacturing is still the leading business activity, yet computers and other electronics are now the top factory goods. That includes military communications equipment and scientific instruments.

Other factories make machinery and metal goods. New Hampshire also has a busy wood industry. Its forests provide wood for furniture, paper, and other wood products.

Many New Hampshire workers hold service jobs. They may be computer programmers, teachers, or lawyers. Some work in restaurants, hotels, hospitals, or banks. Many workers serve skiers, campers, and other visitors. This is important because tourism is a big business in the state. It's New Hampshire's second-largest industry, after manufacturing. About 26 million people visit New Hampshire every year. They bring billions of dollars into the state's economy.

▲ **This New Hampshire teacher is a service worker, too.**

Until the early 1800s, farming was New Hampshire's main industry. Today, farms cover only a small land area. However, they grow more than $675 million worth of products every year. Most farms are in the Connecticut and Merrimack River valleys. Milk and other dairy products are the leading farm products. New Hampshire cows give more than 40 million gallons (151 million liters) of milk a year! Chickens and eggs are important, too.

Many farmers grow decorative trees and plants. That includes flowers and Christmas trees. Hay is the major field crop. It's grown to feed dairy cows and beef cattle. Some farmers make maple syrup and maple sugar. They make these delicious treats with sap from their maple trees.

▲ Chickens are an important farm product for New Hampshire.

▲ The buckets attached to these trees are used to collect sap for maple syrup.

Every year, New Hampshirites make more than 75,000 gallons (284,000 liters) of maple syrup.

New Hampshire's nickname is the Granite State. Its mountains contain rich supplies of red and gray granite. This stone is used for buildings and monuments. However, sand and gravel are the state's leading minerals.

Whose woods these are I think I know.

His house is in the village though;

He will not see me stopping here

To watch his woods fill up with snow.

The poet Robert Frost wrote these lines. They're from the poem "Stopping by Woods on a Snowy Evening." It's part of Frost's poetry collection called *New Hampshire.*

Frost was one of America's best-loved poets. He lived in New Hampshire for many years. New Hampshirites are proud of Frost. He showed the world how beautiful New England is. His poems also celebrate the quiet strength of local people.

Like other New Englanders, New Hampshirites are often called Yankees. That name comes from the colonial days. Yankees were known for being clever, tough, and practical. They were said to be careful with money. Even today, New Hampshirites are proud of those qualities.

Only nine states have fewer people than New Hampshire. In fact, several U.S. cities have more residents! In 2000, there

▲ Poet Robert Frost in 1913

were 1,235,786 people in New Hampshire. Manchester, Nashua, and Concord are the biggest cities. They are all in the southern half of the state. About half of all New Hampshirites live in city areas. The rest are spread out in less-populated areas.

Many New Hampshirites have descended from early settlers. The first settlers came from England. Later, people came from Scotland, Ireland, Germany, and France. In the late 1800s, many French-Canadians and Europeans arrived. Today, twenty-four out of every twenty-five residents are white. The state has a small number of Asians, **Hispanics,** and African-Americans.

▲ **A colonial village in Canterbury**

▲ An October pumpkin festival in Keene

Winter sports races are popular in New Hampshire. Laconia and Center Sandwich hold sled-dog races in February. There are ski races in the snowy mountains. Music festivals and craft fairs are popular, too. Mount Sunapee hosts the League of New Hampshire Craftsmen's Fair every August. Winter carnivals offer another chance for fun. They're held in Plymouth, Hanover, Franconia, and many other towns. Dartmouth College's carnival in Hanover features huge ice sculptures.

▲ Dartmouth College

Dartmouth is New Hampshire's oldest college. It was founded in 1769. The University of New Hampshire is based in Durham. There are also state colleges in Keene and Plymouth.

Let's Explore New Hampshire!

New Hampshire is a great place to explore! Strawbery Banke in Portsmouth was a colonial seaport. Wealthy shipbuilders lived there. Pirates lurked around there, too. Its homes date from as early as the 1600s. You can watch potters, barrel makers, and other craftspeople at work. The William Pitt Tavern is one of the many historic buildings. It was a meeting house for planning the Revolutionary War.

Hampton Beach runs along the Atlantic Coast. The Seacoast Science Center is in Rye. It explores the seacoast's creatures and land features.

▲ You can learn about pirates and wealthy colonial shipbuilders if you visit Portsmouth's Strawbery Banke Museum.

Awesome stone structures stand in Salem. Ancient people built them more than four thousand years ago. This site is called America's Stonehenge, named after a group of stone monuments in England. Both sites were built to work like a calendar. Certain points line up perfectly with the sun at the change of seasons.

The farm where the poet Robert Frost lived from 1900 to 1911 is in nearby Derry. Visitors can tour his farmhouse and barn.

▲ **One of the stone structures at America's Stonehenge in Salem**

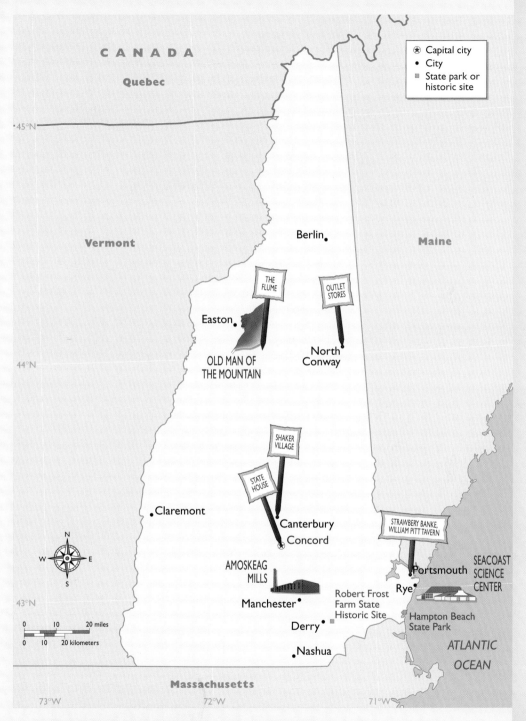

CANADA

Quebec

45°N

Vermont

Maine

Berlin

THE FLUME

OUTLET STORES

Easton

OLD MAN OF THE MOUNTAIN

North Conway

44°N

SHAKER VILLAGE

STATE HOUSE

Claremont

Canterbury

Concord

STRAWBERY BANKE, WILLIAM PITT TAVERN

SEACOAST SCIENCE CENTER

N
W   E
S

AMOSKEAG MILLS

Portsmouth

Rye

43°N

Manchester

Robert Frost Farm State Historic Site

Hampton Beach State Park

ATLANTIC OCEAN

0   10   20 miles
0   10   20 kilometers

Derry

Nashua

Massachusetts

73°W

72°W

71°W

Capital city
City
State park or historic site

▲ **Places to visit in New Hampshire**

▲ **Mount Monadnock is surrounded by the beautiful New England countryside.**

Mount Monadnock is said to be the most-climbed mountain in North America. Some people even say it's the most-climbed peak in the world! Thousands of people hike up its cool, wooded slopes every year. From the top, they gaze down across the New England countryside.

Manchester was once known for its cotton mills. Its massive old Amoskeag Mills buildings still stand. The capitol's golden dome shines over Concord, the state capital. Take a tour inside. You can watch the state's lawmakers at work.

Shaker Village is in Canterbury. Members of the Shaker religion settled there in the 1700s. You'll see traditional Shaker crafts such as furniture making. You can also try Shaker food.

▲ A sign for Shaker Village in Canterbury

More than fifty covered bridges are scattered throughout the state. Settlers originally built the bridges out of wood. For protection, "barns," or roofs, were built over them. Cornish-Windsor Bridge is the longest covered bridge in America. It's almost 450 feet (137 meters) long. It spans the Connecticut River between Cornish and Vermont.

Lake Winnipesaukee, the state's largest lake, is at the southern end of the White Mountains. It's a popular spot for boating and swimming.

▲ A covered bridge along the Kancamagus Highway in the White Mountains

Do you like to shop 'till you drop? Then head north of the lake to North Conway. It's jammed with outlet stores. You'll get great discounts on designer clothing. As an added bonus, New Hampshire has no sales tax. That attracts many businesses—and people—to the state.

▲ A leather store in North Conway

There's a lot to explore in the White Mountains. If you like hiking, try the Appalachian Trail. This path runs down the eastern United States. In New Hampshire, it winds through the White Mountains.

Near Easton perched the state's emblem and most famous "face." It was the Old Man of the Mountain, the side of the mountain that looked like a human face. Nathaniel Hawthorne made it famous in his story "The Great Stone Face." It's about a boy who admired the face's noble qualities. He grew up to have those qualities himself. Unfortunately, the rock profile

▲ **A trail in Franconia Notch State Park**

fell off the mountain in May 2003.

Profile Lake reflects the mountain. This glassy lake was created by an ancient glacier. Nearby is a deep, narrow **gorge** called the Flume. You can take a trail along its damp cliff sides. Glaciers also formed the Glacial Caverns of Lost River. To the north, in Franconia, is another farm of Robert Frost's. Walk along the "poetry nature trail." You'll pass sites that inspired many of his poems.

Mount Washington is New Hampshire's highest peak. You can ride a little train to the top. On a clear day you'll see New Hampshire, Maine, Vermont, New York, and Canada.

Far-northern New Hampshire is often called the Great North Woods. One famous little town there is Dixville Notch. It's proud to be the "first of the first" to vote on primary election day. Just before midnight, residents gather in a voting room. At the stroke of midnight, they cast their votes. It takes just a couple of minutes to count them and announce the results!

▲ The first vote of the 2000 New Hampshire primary was cast in Dixville Notch.

▲ Autumn in White Mountains National Forest

You could spend days wandering through the Great North Woods. Lakes, ponds, and sparkling streams are nestled in its wooded valleys.

American history is nestled in these woods as well. Explore the past and the present in New Hampshire. It's a beautiful state.

Important Dates

1623 British colonists make New Hampshire's first permanent settlements at present-day Rye and Dover.

1641 New Hampshire settlements become part of the Massachusetts Colony.

1680 New Hampshire becomes a British royal colony.

1776 On January 5, New Hampshire adopts its own constitution.

1788 New Hampshire becomes the ninth state on June 21.

1853 New Hampshirite Franklin Pierce becomes the fourteenth U.S. president.

1905 The treaty ending the Russo-Japanese War is signed in Portsmouth.

1929 Sig Buchmayr opens the first American ski school on Sugar Hill.

1944 The International Monetary Conference is held at Bretton Woods.

1961 New Hampshirite Alan B. Shepard Jr. is the first U.S. astronaut in space.

1986 Concord schoolteacher and astronaut Christa McAuliffe is killed when the space shuttle *Challenger* explodes shortly after takeoff.

1990 David Souter of New Hampshire joins the U.S. Supreme Court.

1996 Jeanne Shaheen is the first woman elected governor of New Hampshire.

2003 The rocks of the Old Man of the Mountain fall off the mountainside.

Glossary

candidate—someone running for office in an election

colonists—people who settle a new land for their home country

colonies—territories that belong to the country that settles them

glaciers—huge sheets of ice that move slowly

gorge—a deep, narrow valley

granite—a hard stone used for buildings and monuments

Hispanics—people of Mexican, South American, and other Spanish-speaking cultures

incorporated—joined together in a single whole

terms—periods of time in office that are determined by law

Did You Know?

★ Besides New Hampshire, the New England states are Maine, Massachusetts, Vermont, Rhode Island, and Connecticut.

★ New Hampshire is sometimes called the Mother of Rivers. Five of New England's great rivers rise there. They are the Connecticut, Merrimack, Piscataqua, Androscoggin, and Saco Rivers.

★ In 2000, these cities had a larger population than the entire state of New Hampshire: New York, New York; Los Angeles, California; Chicago, Illinois; Houston, Texas; Philadelphia, Pennsylvania; and Phoenix, Arizona.

★ To go into effect, the U.S. Constitution needed the approval of at least nine former colonies. As the ninth colony to vote yes, New Hampshire cast the deciding vote.

★ Who wrote "Mary Had a Little Lamb"? It was Sarah Josepha Hale of Newport, New Hampshire. She wrote the poem in 1830.

★ It takes about 40 gallons (151 liters) of maple sap to make 1 gallon (3.8 liters) of maple syrup.

★ New Hampshire's state legislature has 424 members. Only the United States, the United Kingdom, and India have larger legislatures!

★ John Mason named New Hampshire after his home county of Hampshire in England.

At a Glance

State capital: Concord

State motto: Live Free or Die

State nickname: The Granite State

Statehood: June 21, 1788; ninth state

Land area: 8,969 square miles (23,230 sq km); **rank:** forty-fourth

Highest point: Mount Washington, 6,288 feet (1,917 m) above sea level

Lowest point: Sea level, along the Atlantic coast

Highest recorded temperature: 106°F (41°C) at Nashua on July 4, 1911

Lowest recorded temperature: −47°F (−44°C) at Mount Washington on January 29, 1934

Average January temperature: 19°F (−7°C)

Average July temperature: 68°F (20°C)

Population in 2000: 1,235,786; **rank:** forty-first

Largest cities in 2000: Manchester (107,006), Nashua (86,605), Concord (40,687), Derry (34,021)

Factory products: Machinery, electrical equipment, scientific instruments

Farm products: Milk, hay, apples

Mining products: Sand, gravel, granite

State flag: New Hampshire's state flag

shows the state seal on a field of blue. Around the seal are laurel branches and nine stars. The stars represent New Hampshire's place as the ninth state to join the Union.

State seal: The state seal shows the Revolutionary War ship *Raleigh*

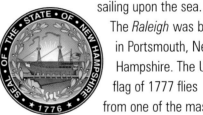

sailing upon the sea. The *Raleigh* was built in Portsmouth, New Hampshire. The U.S. flag of 1777 flies from one of the masts. In the background, the sun is rising. In the front is a granite boulder. It stands for the Granite State's most famous mineral. A laurel wreath encircles this scene. Around the edge are the words, "Seal of the State of New Hampshire" and the date "1776."

State emblem: The state emblem is a design of the Old Man of the Mountain. This famous natural landmark stood over Echo Lake. Around this design are the words "State of New Hampshire" and the state motto, "Live Free or Die."

State abbreviations: N.H. (traditional); NH (postal)

State Symbols

State bird: Purple finch

State flower: Purple lilac

State tree: White birch

State wildflower: Pink lady's slipper

State animal: White-tailed deer

State freshwater fish: Brook trout

State saltwater game fish: Striped bass

State amphibian: Spotted newt

State insect: Ladybug

State butterfly: Karner blue

State mineral: Beryl

State rock: Granite

State gem: Smoky quartz

State sport: Skiing

State commemorative quarter:
Released on August 7, 2000

Making Maple Syrup Pie

One of New Hampshire's many delicious maple syrup treats.

Makes eight to ten servings.

INGREDIENTS:

I cup maple syrup
(New Hampshirites say theirs is best!)

1/2 cup water

3 teaspoons cornstarch

2 teaspoons cold water

2 egg yolks

2 teaspoons butter or margarine

1/4 cup chopped nuts

I ready-made pie crust

DIRECTIONS:

Make sure an adult helps you with the hot stove. Preheat the oven to 400°F. Mix the syrup and the 1/2 cup water in a pan. Bring to a low boil and simmer for about 5 minutes. Meanwhile, mix the cornstarch in the cold water until it's like paste. Add egg yolks and beat well. Add to the syrup mixture. Keep cooking over low heat, and stir as you cook. When it gets thick, add the butter and nuts. Remove from heat and let it cool. Then pour it into the pie crust. Bake for 25 to 30 minutes. Chill before serving.

"Old New Hampshire"

Words by Dr. John F. Holmes, music by Maurice Hoffmann

With a skill that knows no measure,
From the golden store of Fate
God, in His great love and wisdom,
Made the rugged Granite State;
Made the lakes, the fields, the forests;
Made the Rivers and the rills;
Made the bubbling, crystal fountains
Of New Hampshire's Granite Hills.

Chorus:
Old New Hampshire, Old New Hampshire
Old New Hampshire Grand and Great
We will sing of Old New Hampshire,
Of the dear old Granite State.

Builded he New Hampshire glorious
From the borders to the sea;
And with matchless charm and splendor
Blessed her for eternity.
Hers, the majesty of mountain;
Hers, the grandeur of the lake;
Hers, the truth as from the hillside
Whence her crystal waters break.

Chorus:
Old New Hampshire, Old New Hampshire
Old New Hampshire Grand and Great
We will sing of Old New Hampshire,
Of the dear old Granite State.

Salmon P. Chase (1808–1873) was chief justice of the U.S. Supreme Court (1864–1873). As a lawyer, he defended many runaway slaves.

Mary Baker Eddy (1821–1910) was a religious leader. She founded the Christian Science religion and the *Christian Science Monitor* newspaper.

Robert Frost (1874–1963) was a poet. Many of his poems tell of the beauty of New England. Born in California, Frost (pictured above left) lived for many years in New Hampshire.

Horace Greeley (1811–1872) was a newspaper editor and social reformer. He worked to abolish slavery. Greeley founded the *New York Tribune.*

John Irving (1942–) is an author. His books include *The World According to Garp, The Hotel New Hampshire,* and *The Cider House Rules.* All three were made into popular movies.

Sharon Christa McAuliffe (1948–1986) was a Concord teacher. On the space shuttle *Challenger,* she and all other crew members died when the spacecraft exploded. She was born in Massachusetts.

Edward MacDowell (1860–1908) was a pianist and composer. He was born in New York and kept a summer home in Peterborough.

Franklin Pierce (1804–1869) was the fourteenth U.S. president (1853–1857).

J. D. Salinger (1919–) is an author. His most famous book is *Catcher in the Rye.* Salinger was born in New York and moved to Cornish. J. D. stands for Jerome David.

Alan Shepard Jr. (1923–1998) was the first American astronaut in space. He made this flight in 1961 aboard the *Freedom 7.* Later, he commanded the *Apollo 14* mission to the Moon.

David Souter (1939–) became a justice of the U.S. Supreme Court in 1990. He was born in Massachusetts.

John Stark (1728–1822) was a Revolutionary War hero. He led the colonists to victory in the Battle of Bennington (1777). His words became New Hampshire's state motto: "Live free or die."

Harlan Fiske Stone (1872–1946) joined the U.S. Supreme Court in 1925. He served as chief justice from 1941 to 1946.

John Sununu (1939–) was governor of New Hampshire (1983–1989) and chief of staff for President George Bush (1989–1991). He was born in Cuba.

Daniel Webster (1782–1852) was a political leader and a powerful speaker. He was U.S. secretary of state twice (1841–1843) and (1850–1852). Before the Civil War, he fought to preserve the Union but angered antislavery groups.

Want to Know More?

At the Library

Blos, Joan W. *A Gathering of Days.* New York: Aladdin Paperbacks, 1990.

Brown, Dottie. *New Hampshire.* Minneapolis: Lerner, 1993.

Bruchac, Joseph. *The Heart of a Chief.* New York: Dial Books for Young Readers, 1998.

Italia, Bob. *New Hampshire Colony.* Edina, Minn.: Checkerboard Library, 2002.

Shannon, Terry Miller. *New Hampshire.* Danbury, Conn.: Children's Press, 2002.

Thompson, Kathleen. *New Hampshire.* Austin, Tex.: Raintree/Steck Vaughn, 1996.

Welsbacher, Anne. *New Hampshire.* Edina, Minn.: Abdo & Daughters, 1998.

On the Web

New Hampshire State Government Online

http://www.state.nh.us/
To learn about New Hampshire's history, government, economy, and land

New Hampshire Tourism

http://www.visitnh.gov
To find out about New Hampshire's events, activities, and sights

New Hampshire Almanac

http://www.state.nh.us/nhinfo/index.html
For information on New Hampshire's people, wildlife, government, and more

Through the Mail

New Hampshire Division of Travel and Tourism Development

172 Pembroke Road
P.O. Box 1856
Concord, NH 03302
For information on travel and interesting sights in New Hampshire

New Hampshire Historical Society

The Tuck Library
30 Park Street
Concord, NH 03301
603/228-6688
For information on New Hampshire's history

On the Road

New Hampshire State House

107 North Main Street
Concord, NH 03301
603/271-2154
To visit New Hampshire's state capitol

Index

About the Author

Ann Heinrichs grew up in Fort Smith, Arkansas, and lives in Chicago. She is the author of more than one hundred books for children and young adults on Asian, African, and U.S. history and culture. Ann has also written numerous newspaper, magazine, and encyclopedia articles. She is an award-winning martial artist, specializing in t'ai chi empty-hand and sword forms.

Ann has traveled widely throughout the United States, Africa, Asia, and the Middle East. In exploring each state for this series, she rediscovered the people, history, and resources that make this a great land, as well as the concerns we share with people around the world.